Engaging God's Word

Ruth and Esther

Engage Bible Studies

Tools That Transform

Engage Bible Studies
an imprint of

Engaging God's Word: Ruth and Esther

ISBN 978-1-62194-017-3

Published by Community Bible Study
790 Stout Road
Colorado Springs, CO
1-800-826-4181
www.communitybiblestudy.org

Printed in the United States of America.

Contents

Introduction

Welcome to the life-changing adventure of engaging with God's Word! Whether this is the first time you've opened a Bible or you've studied the Scriptures all your life, good things are in store for you. Studying the Bible is unlike any other kind of study you have ever done. That's because the Word of God is *"living and active"* (Hebrews 4:12) and transcends time and cultures. The earth and heavens as we know them will one day pass away, but God's Word never will (Mark 13:31). It's as relevant to your life today as it was to the people who wrote it down centuries ago. And the fact that God's Word is living and active means that reading God's Word is always meant to be a personal experience. God's Word is not just dead words on a page—it is page after page of living, powerful words—so get ready, because the time you spend studying the Bible in this *Engaging God's Word* course will be life-transforming!

Why Study the Bible?

Some Christians read the Bible because they know they're supposed to. It's a good thing to do, and God expects it. And all that's true! However, there are many additional reasons to study God's Word. Here are just some of them.

We get to know God through His Word. Our God is a relational God who knows us and wants us to know Him. The Scriptures, which He authored, reveal much about Him: how He thinks and feels, what His purposes are, what He thinks about us, how He views the world He made, what He has planned for the future. The Bible shows us God's many attributes—His kindness, goodness, justice, love, faithfulness, mercy, compassion, creativity, redemption, sovereignty, and so on. As we get to know Him through His Word, we come to love and trust Him.

God speaks to us through His Word. One of the primary ways God speaks to us is through His written Word. Don't be surprised if, as you read the Bible, certain parts nearly jump off the page at you, almost as if they'd been written with you in mind. God is the Author of this incredible book, so that's not just possible, it's likely! Whether it is to find comfort, warning, correction, teaching, or guidance, always approach God's Word with your spiritual ears open (Isaiah 55:3) because God, your loving heavenly Father, has things He wants to say to you.

God's Word brings life. Just about everyone wants to learn the secret to "the good life." And the good news is, that secret is found in God's Word. Don't think of the Bible as a bunch of rules. Viewing it with that mindset is a distortion. God gave us His Word because as our Creator and the Creator of the universe, He alone knows how life was meant to work. He knows that love makes us happier than hate, that generosity brings more joy than greed, and that integrity allows us to rest more peacefully at night than deception does. God's ways are not always "easiest" but they are the way to life. As the Psalmist says, *"If Your law had not been my delight, I would have perished in my affliction. I will never forget Your precepts, for by them You have given me life"* (Psalm 119:92-93).

God's Word offers stability in an unstable world. Truth is an ever-changing negotiable for many people in our culture today. But building your life on constantly changing "truth" is like building your house on shifting sand. God's Word, like God Himself, never changes. What He says was true yesterday, is true today, and will still be true a billion years from now. Jesus said, *"Everyone then who hears these words of Mine and does them will be like a wise man who built his house on the rock"* (Matthew 7:24).

God's Word helps us to pray effectively. When we read God's Word and get to know what He is really like, we understand better how to pray. God answers prayers that are according to His will. We discover His will by reading the Bible. First John 5:14-15 tells us that *"this is the confidence that we have toward Him, that if we ask anything according to His will He hears us. And if we know that He hears us in whatever we ask, we know that we have the requests that we have asked of Him."*

How to Get the Most out of *Engaging God's Word*

Each *Engaging God's Word* study contains key elements that have been carefully designed to help you get the most out of your time in God's Word. Slightly modified for your study-at-home success, this approach is very similar to the tried-and-proven Bible study method that Community Bible Study has used with thousands of men, women, and children across the United States and around the world for nearly 40 years. There are some basic things you can expect to find in each course in this series.

- Lesson 1 provides an overview of the Bible book (or books) you will study and questions to help you focus, anticipate, and pray about what you will be learning.
- Every lesson contains questions to answer on your own, commentary that reviews and clarifies the passage, and three special sections called "Apply what you have learned," "Think about" and "Personalize this lesson."
- Some lessons contain memory verse suggestions.

Whether you plan to use *Engaging God's Word* on your own or with a group, here are some suggestions that will help you enjoy and receive the most benefit from your study.

Spread out each lesson over several days. Your *Engaging God's Word* lessons were designed to take a week to complete. Spreading out your study rather than doing it all at once allows time for the things God is teaching you to sink in and for you to practice applying them.

Pray each time you read God's Word. The Bible is a book unlike any other because God Himself inspired it. The same Spirit who inspired the human authors who wrote it will help you to understand and apply it if you ask Him to. So make it a practice to ask Him to make His Word come alive to you every time you read it.

Read the whole passage covered in the lesson. Before plunging into the questions, take time to read the specific chapter or verses that will be covered in that lesson. Doing this will give you important context for the whole lesson. Reading the Bible in context is an important principle in interpreting it accurately.

Begin learning the memory verse. Learning Scripture by heart requires discipline, but the rewards far outweigh the effort. Memorizing a verse allows you to recall it whenever you need it—for personal encouragement and direction, or to share with someone else. Consider writing the verse on a sticky note or index card that you can post where you will see it often or carry with you to review during the day. Reading and re-reading the verse often—out loud when possible—is a simple way to commit it to memory.

Re-read the passage for each section of questions. Each lesson is divided into sections so that you study one small part of Scripture at a time. Before attempting to answer the questions, review the verses that the questions will cover.

Answer the questions without consulting the Commentary or other reference materials. There is great joy in having the Holy Spirit teach you God's Word on your own, without the help of outside resources. Don't cheat yourself of the delight of discovery by reading the Commentary prematurely. Wait until after you've completed the lesson.

Repeat the process for all the question sections.

Prayerfully consider the "Apply what you have learned," marked with the push pin symbol. The vision of Community Bible Study is not to just gain knowledge about the Bible, but to be transformed by it. For this reason, each set of questions closes with a section that encourages you to apply what you are learning. Usually this section involves action—something for you to do. As you practice these suggestions, your life will change.

Read the Commentary. *Engaging God's Word* commentaries are written by theologians whose goal is to help you understand the context of what you are studying as it relates to the rest of Scripture, God's character, and what the passage means for your life. Of necessity, the commentaries include the author's interpretations. While interesting and helpful, keep in mind that the Commentary is simply one person's understanding of what these passages mean. Other godly men and women have views that are also worth considering.

Pause to contemplate each "Think about" section, marked with the notepad symbol. These features, embedded in the Commentary, offer a place to pause and consider some of the principles being brought out by the text. They provide excellent ideas to journal about or to discuss with other believers, especially those doing the study with you.

Jot down insights or prayer points from the "Personalize this lesson" marked with the ☑ check box symbol. While the "Apply what you have learned" section focuses on doing, the "Personalize this lesson" section focuses on becoming. Spiritual transformation is not just about doing right things and refraining from doing wrong things—it is about changing from the inside out. To be transformed means letting God change our hearts so that our attitudes, emotions, desires, reactions, and goals are increasingly like Jesus'. Often this section will discuss something that you cannot do in your own strength—so your response will usually be something to pray about. Remember that becoming more Christ-like is not just a matter of trying harder—it requires God's empowerment.

Overview

Ruth and Esther

The books of Ruth and Esther both tell stories of ordinary people, which play out against the backdrop of God's character and work. Both books feature women as the main characters. While these stories have often been romanticized, we can't miss that these women endure terrible loss and devastation.

The book of Ruth tells of Naomi and Ruth, a mother- and daughter-in-law. Naomi is a refugee from famine. She has not only buried her husband but also mourned the deaths of both of her grown sons. Her daughter-in-law, Ruth, is a young widow torn between leaving her country and home or losing her beloved mother-in-law. As widows without a means of support, they both knew poverty, hardship, and uncertain futures.

Esther faces possibly even worse circumstances. Displaced by war, she has been drafted into a pagan king's harem, forever denied a normal family life with a husband and children—and is required to make a decision that could cost her life.

Yet in both books, something bigger than hardship and personal drama is in play. They are rare among Bible books in that God's role is decidedly in the background. In other books, we see Him speaking to His people, sending prophets, and actively moving and delivering. Not here. Though people in the book of Ruth refer to God, His overt activity is nowhere to be found. And the book of Esther never mentions God at all. Even so, He is still at work behind the scenes. Both of these books exemplify God's providence.

Providence comes from a Latin expression that means "to see ahead"—the idea of foresight. When we speak of God's providence, we mean that He is sustaining everything He has created, and He is guiding and working toward His good and perfect plans.

God upholds and sustains the entire world (Colossians 1:17). He sets up and deposes rulers and rearranges kingdoms (Psalm 22:28; Daniel 4:34-35). And He works individually in people's lives, determining where they should live (Acts 17:26-27), directing events (Psalm 139:16), and maintaining intimate knowledge and care of them (Luke 12:6-7).

God's work in these ways is fully displayed in both of these books. The book of Ruth highlights the lives of very ordinary people in a small village during the time of Judges. Amid widespread disregard for God and His laws, here we see a pocket of people following God and obeying the provisions of His law. What they do not know is that God is also actively caring for them and bringing about events for their good. What's more, through them He is establishing the line of succession not only for the future King David, but also for the Messiah Himself.

The book of Esther takes place centuries later when the Jewish people are in exile in the Persian Empire, suffering the results of widespread disobedience to God. In this book, we again see the lives of two very ordinary people, Mordecai and Esther, who are in exactly the right places at exactly the right times. They face hardship with courage and humility, and God rewards them as a result. Their personal story plays out in the context of the larger story of God's deliverance for the entire Jewish population. Even though He is judging the people for their sin against Him, God is also providentially protecting and preserving them.

Both of these books are highlighted at Jewish holidays—for good reason. The book of Ruth is read at Shavuot (the Festival of Weeks) and Esther is read at Purim. These stories celebrate the care and goodness of our providential God both on a personal level and in the broader scope of human events.

1. Have you ever experienced a time when it appeared God was not at work, but you later found out "the rest of the story"? What happened?

____

____

____

____

2. When circumstances make it appear that God is not actively intervening, what assumptions might people make about Him?

3. How do you typically respond when your life circumstances do not seem to indicate God is near and active?

4. What perspective might applying the truth of God's providence lead you to?

5. Consider a person facing great hardship who yet remains true to God. How might this person's faithfulness affect God—what might He feel about this person?

If you are doing this study with a group, take time to pray for one another. Ask God to reveal Himself as you work through this study each week, so that you increasingly notice how He is present, active, and caring for each one of you. If you are doing this study on your own, ask God how He would want you to be aware of His attentive care, and how you can respond to that care. Write your prayer below.

Lesson 1

Ruth and Naomi

Ruth 1

Memorize God's Word: Psalm 46:1.

❖ Ruth 1—Overview of Ruth's Life

1. According to verse 1, in what period of Jewish history does this story take place?

2. Read the final verse of the book of Judges (21:25). How does the tone or mood of the first chapter of Ruth show signs of the times in which the events took place?

❖ Ruth 1:1-5—Naomi Faces Great Loss

3. Who is Naomi, and where is her home?

4. Why does her family leave?

5. Why were the Moabites not conquered by the Israelites? (See Deuteronomy 2:9.)

6. What had happened when the Israelites had previously associated with the Moabites? (See Numbers 25:1-3.)

7. See Deuteronomy 23:3-6. What other alienation from Israel was pronounced on Moab?

8. Why do you think Elimelech and his family risk association with these people?

❖ Ruth 1:6-14—Naomi Decides to Leave Moab

9. Why does Naomi decide to return to Bethlehem?

10. What does verse 6 tell you about God's relationship to His people? (See Exodus 4:31.)

11. Why do you think Naomi tries to convince her daughters-in-law not to go with her?

12. What blessing does she give them?

13. Why does she think it futile for them to return with her? (See Deuteronomy 25:5-6.)

14. What is Naomi's attitude toward God? Toward her daughters-in-law?

15. How do the two women respond?

❖ Ruth 1:15-18—Ruth Decides to Go With Naomi

16. What does Ruth's response reveal about her feelings toward Naomi? Her commitment to God?

17. Remember Ruth's background and position. What does Isaiah 56:6-8 tell us about why and how God responds to Ruth?

18. Why and how does God respond to people in similar situations today? (See Acts 10:34-35.)

❖ Ruth 1:19-22—Ruth and Naomi Arrive in Bethlehem

19. How do the townspeople react to Naomi's return?

____

____

20. List the words Naomi uses to describe her condition.

____

____

21. What has her affliction done to her faith?

____

____

22. What had these afflictions done to Ruth's faith?

____

____

23. Read Job 1:13-22 and summarize what had happened to Job. How did he respond to his situation? Compare his response to Naomi's?

____

____

Apply what you have learned. No matter how bad a circumstance may feel, we need not despair if we are children of God. He has promised that He will be with us, and He is our hope. "May the God of hope fill you with all joy and peace in believing, so that by the power of the Holy Spirit you may abound in hope" (Romans 15:13). If you are in a season of loss, ask God to help you experience His nearness and care even in the midst of your struggle and pain.

Lesson 1 Commentary

Ruth and Naomi

Ruth 1

Introduction

During the chaotic period of the Judges, some Israelites do trust and follow God. The book of Ruth describes how God guided such a family in the humble village of Bethlehem. A Jew and a Gentile marry and become ancestors of King David, from whom the Messiah will come (Matthew 1:5-16). Ruth's Moabite background establishes the universality of the Messiah—that He will not only be the Savior of Israel, but of *all* people.

The book of Ruth is part of the *Megilloth* (Five Scrolls)—the Song of Solomon, Ruth, Lamentations, Ecclesiastes, and Esther. Jews read the book at the Feast of Harvest (Feast of Weeks), later called the Feast of Pentecost. The book shows the providence of God, that virtue is rewarded (2:11-12), the importance of diligence (2:6-7), and the importance of commitment to one's family (1:17). It is also an invaluable record of the genealogy of King David and Jesus Christ (4:17-22). Many Bible scholars think Samuel wrote this book; others believe it was written early in the reign of King David.

Naomi and Her Family

Naomi and Elimelech live in Judah with their sons, Mahlon and Kilion. During a severe famine, the family moves to Moab. The Moabites had descended from Abraham's nephew Lot through Lot's incestuous encounter with his daughter (Genesis 19:36-37). The Lord had given their land to Lot's descendants (Deuteronomy 2:9). The Moabite King Balak asked a false prophet, Balaam, to curse the Israelites (Numbers 22:4-6, 21-35). Failing to thwart the Israelites through Balaam, the Moabites sought to seduce them into sexual immorality and idolatry.

Succumbing to these temptations proved devastating for the Israelites then (Numbers 25) and throughout their history. King David later conquered the Moabites (2 Samuel 8:2).

Elimelech and his two grown sons die in Moab, leaving Naomi alone with her daughters-in-law, Ruth and Orpah. Hearing that the famine in Israel is over, they plan to return to Judah. However, Naomi urges Ruth and Orpah to go back to their mothers' homes. It is clear from her words in verse 8 that these two women have been faithful wives and daughters-in-law who love her.

Unless they were independently wealthy, women at that time needed males—a father, a brother, or a husband—to support them. Ruth and Orpah must need such help. At first, both insist on going with Naomi, who paints a hopeless picture of their future. The levirate (the Latin levir means brother-in-law) marriage provision states: *"If brothers dwell together, and one of them dies and has no son, the wife of the dead man shall not be married outside the family to a stranger. Her husband's brother shall go in to her and take her as his wife and perform the duty of a husband's brother to her. And the first son whom she bears shall succeed to the name of his dead brother, that his name may not be blotted out of Israel"* (Deuteronomy 25:5-6). Naomi says she has no way of providing husbands for them and that God's hand is against her. However, we will see that God does care for Naomi through the faithfulness of a loving daughter-in-law and a kindhearted relative.

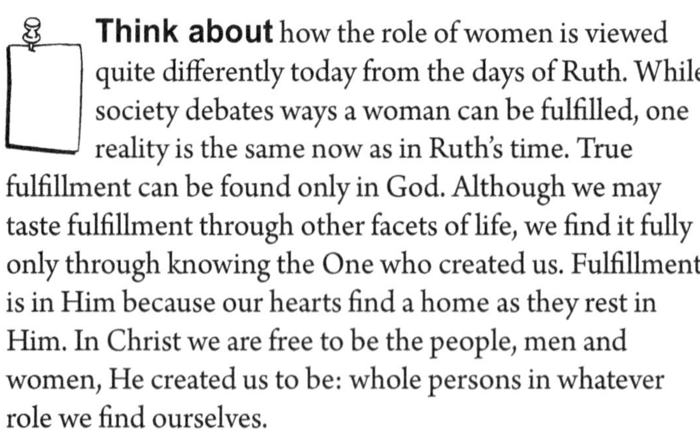

Think about how the role of women is viewed quite differently today from the days of Ruth. While society debates ways a woman can be fulfilled, one reality is the same now as in Ruth's time. True fulfillment can be found only in God. Although we may taste fulfillment through other facets of life, we find it fully only through knowing the One who created us. Fulfillment is in Him because our hearts find a home as they rest in Him. In Christ we are free to be the people, men and women, He created us to be: whole persons in whatever role we find ourselves.

Naomi and Ruth

Naomi convinces Orpah not to go with her. Ruth, however, *"clung to"* her (1:14). The Hebrew word for *cling* is *dabaq,* meaning *cleave unto, adhere to.* That word is used in Genesis 2:24 to describe the bond between man and wife. Ruth is committed to Naomi until death, regardless of the effects on her own life. Naomi again tries to persuade Ruth not to go with her, but Ruth pleads, *"Do not urge me to leave you or to return from following you. For where you go I will go, and where you lodge I will lodge. Your people shall be my people, and your God my God"* (1:16). These words paint a graphic picture of the meaning of *to cleave.* Ruth had determined to follow Naomi anywhere, knowing it included worship of Naomi's God (1:16-17). When she says *"May the LORD do so to me,"* she uses the word Yahweh for God, which indicates that she already trusts in Him.

Naomi accepts her decision, and together they travel to Bethlehem. When the townspeople see her, they ask, *"Is this Naomi?"* Naomi asks people not to call her Naomi but *Mara, bitter.* It has indeed been a bitter ordeal to lose her husband and two sons in a strange land.

Think about this: Who has not experienced troubles? We can identify with Naomi, because we have also had times of affliction. But we do not have to grieve like those *"who have no hope"* (1 Thessalonians 4:13)? The One who is *"the resurrection and the life"* (John 11:25) is our constant companion. Let us focus upon Him and be open to His *"peace ... which surpasses all understanding"* (Philippians 4:7). When we encounter loss or adversity, remember that nothing—not even a present tragedy—can separate us from the love of God in Christ Jesus (Romans 8:38-39). As we abide in Him, He will lovingly lift us. He is the Giver of lasting peace, our true Comforter and Restorer.

In God's providence, Ruth arrives with Naomi at the beginning of the barley harvest, as Israel is commemorating the Passover. As we will see in chapters 2–4, God will meet her every need—physical as well as spiritual. His plan for her was more wonderful than anything she could have imagined.

Personalize this lesson.

☑ Ruth and Naomi are wonderful role models. In Ruth we see the qualities of faithfulness, loyalty, and compassion. She loved Naomi and longed to be with her. Ruth would not have gone to an unfamiliar place to live among strangers except for Naomi. What Ruth understood about God, she understood because of Naomi. As for Naomi, although she felt sad and empty, she wanted joyful, complete lives for Ruth and Orpah and prayed for God's blessings to rest upon them. In her time of affliction and calamity, Naomi showed love and concern for others. Although she thought of herself as having a bitter life, there was obviously something about her—a sweetness and warmth—that caused Ruth to love her. What are some steps you can take to build greater faithfulness toward those close to you? List a few of the unique ways God has created you to demonstrate love to others. Ask Him to give you an opportunity to exercise one of these gifts during the next week. Then watch for your chance!

Lesson 2

Ruth and Boaz

Ruth 2–4

Memorize God's Word: Ruth 1:16.

❖ Ruth 2:1-7—Ruth Gleans in Boaz's Field

1. Who is Boaz?

2. What do the greetings between Boaz and his reapers tell you about their relationship to God and to one another?

3. What steps does Ruth take to provide food for herself and Naomi?

4. Why is she able to take such actions? (See Leviticus 23:22.)

5. What does God promise those who follow this command? (See Deuteronomy 24:19.)

❖ Ruth 2:8-16—Ruth Finds Favor With Boaz

6. What advice does Boaz give Ruth?

7. How does Boaz protect her and care for her needs?

8. What correlation can you see between Boaz's actions and his words in verse 12?

9. Although Boaz has not met Ruth (see verse 5), how and what does he know about her?

10. How can you relate Ruth's experience to Matthew 10:37?

❖ Ruth 2:17–3:5—Naomi and Ruth Develop a Plan

11. From verses 17-21, how does Naomi display a different attitude than she had in 1:21?

12. What is Naomi's plan and why does she believe it is necessary?

❖ Ruth 3:6-18—Ruth Follows Naomi's Plan

13. How and when does Boaz discover Ruth's presence?

14. Why do you think Ruth asks Boaz to spread his wings over her? (See Ezekiel 16:8 and Deuteronomy 25:5.)

15. How does Boaz approve Ruth and accept responsibility for her?

16. How does Naomi's advice to Ruth in verse 18 contain an important message for us?

❖ Ruth 4—Ruth and Boaz Are Married

17. Boaz is called Ruth's *"redeemer."* How could Christ be called our redeemer? (See Philippians 2:7-8; 1 Peter 1:18-21.)

18. Why does the nearest redeemer not redeem Ruth?

19. What do you see regarding your own salvation when you compare the nearest redeemer's actions, Boaz's actions, and the actions described in Galatians 2:16?

20. When Ruth's son is born, how do the women acknowledge his importance to Naomi?

21. Boaz expressed a hope that God would bless and reward Ruth (2:12; 3:10). Write one or two sentences summarizing how his hope was fulfilled.

22. How was the hope fulfilled for all time? (See Matthew 1:3-6.)

23. How would you relate everything that happened to Naomi and Ruth to the truths declared in Romans 8:28?

Apply what you have learned. Like Ruth, let us come to God for refuge. He is our stronghold in the day of trouble, our security in an unstable world. We experience rest as we share our hearts with Him, pour out our thoughts and feelings, and hand over our burdens to His care. Is there a time you have had to do this? What was the experience like for you? How did you come to know God better during this time? Remembering and commemorating what God has done for us can solidify our ability to trust Him during times of ongoing uncertainty.

Lesson 2 Commentary

Ruth and Boaz

Ruth 2–4

Ruth, the Willing Worker

God's care for His people is shown by the fact that Naomi and Ruth arrive in Bethlehem during the barley harvest. Ruth takes the initiative to find food and goes out to collect leftover grain. Harvest gleanings are to be left for the poor to gather (Leviticus 23:22), and everyone benefits. God blesses landowners as they share their harvest (Deuteronomy 24:19), and the gleanings feed the poor. In God's providence, Ruth comes to the field of Boaz, a wealthy relative of Elimelech. Being closely related to Naomi through marriage, Boaz (or another closer relative) is obligated to take care of them (see Leviticus 25:25).

Boaz, a godly man who greets his workers with a blessing and receives a blessing in return, acts kindly toward Ruth. He knows of Ruth's good reputation even before he meets her. Her appeal goes beyond outward appearance; she has a humble, grateful spirit. Like Abraham, she has the courage to go into an unknown situation (Hebrews 11:8-9) because of her confidence in Israel's God. Although her circumstances seem bleak, she believes she can find refuge in God. Boaz, apparently much older than Ruth, treats her protectively, like a daughter. He offers her lunch with his servant girls, telling his workers to let her glean among them and drop grain for her to pick up.

Ruth's Loving Obedience

The close relationship between Ruth and Naomi is evident: Ruth keeps some lunch to share with Naomi and confides everything that happened in the field. Concerned that as long as her daughter-in-law remains a widow with an unsure future she will not be happy, Naomi asks, *"My daughter, should I not seek rest for you, that it may be well with you?"* (3:1).

In spite of her sorrow, Naomi is concerned for Ruth's welfare. We should remember that despondency, such as Naomi experienced, will often lessen as we reach out to help someone else.

In that culture, it is the responsibility of the nearest kinsman to care for a widow by marrying her, if necessary, as well as providing for her. Deuteronomy 25:5-10 states that if a brother died childless, his widow should not marry outside the family. Boaz is in the line of potential redeemers. Naomi's instructions to Ruth should not be viewed as tactics to trap Boaz into marriage. They would merely remind him of the existing situation and his possible duty to do something about it.

Ruth responds to her mother-in-law's plan. She knows that Naomi's instructions are appropriate, as they can help fulfill a duty to perpetuate her dead husband's name. She washes and anoints herself with perfume. She goes to the festive scene that follows the threshing and waits until Boaz lies down to sleep.

Why does she uncover his feet? Perhaps so he will awaken because he is cold and notice her. He does wake during the night and is shocked to see her. Ruth identifies herself, asking him to spread the corner of his garment over her. She is really proposing marriage, as this act signifies a man's readiness to marry a woman. This is a significant moment for them both. Boaz responds warmly to Ruth, but says there is a closer redeemer who must have the first opportunity to wed her.

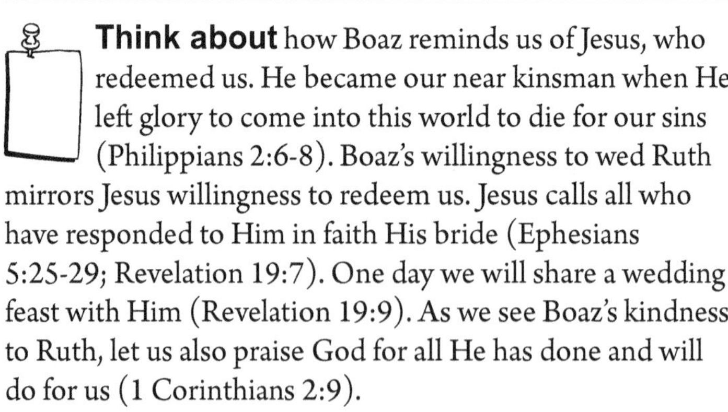

Think about how Boaz reminds us of Jesus, who redeemed us. He became our near kinsman when He left glory to come into this world to die for our sins (Philippians 2:6-8). Boaz's willingness to wed Ruth mirrors Jesus willingness to redeem us. Jesus calls all who have responded to Him in faith His bride (Ephesians 5:25-29; Revelation 19:7). One day we will share a wedding feast with Him (Revelation 19:9). As we see Boaz's kindness to Ruth, let us also praise God for all He has done and will do for us (1 Corinthians 2:9).

Ruth's Reward

Concerned for her reputation, Boaz tells Ruth to leave the threshing floor before she can be recognized. Upon hearing Ruth's report, Naomi wisely advises her to wait patiently. The next day Boaz discusses the situation at the town gate with the closer redeemer before 10 elders (heads of prominent families). A family's welfare is the concern of the entire community, so they want to help Naomi as well as settle legalities with regard to Ruth. Boaz challenges his relative to show his commitment to Naomi's welfare—and Ruth's—by buying Naomi's property for Ruth's heir and providing for Ruth. The man refuses.

Boaz explains everything to the elders. He speaks of "buying" Ruth, but recognizes the distinction between Ruth and the land: she is to be his life partner in the sacred task of building a home (4:10). The elders approve Boaz's intention and ask God's blessings on them. Their reference to Rachel and Leah indicates that these elders know the Pentateuch—unlike many people in the time of the judges. They also mentioned Ephrathah in Bethlehem, which has prophetic significance (see Micah 5:2; Matthew 2:6).

The statement *"the Lord gave her conception, and she bore a son"* (Ruth 4:13) reflects the Hebrew belief that children are a gift from God (see Psalm 127:3-5). The arrival of Obed causes great joy among the women in Bethlehem. Naomi is especially happy. She has already been blessed with a daughter-in-law who is *"more to* [her] *than seven sons"* (4:15). Now she has a secure home and a baby to love. She loved Elimelech; now she can help rear a child who has come from his line. God has indeed been good to Naomi. As for Ruth, she never dreams she will be the ancestress of King David and the Messiah (Matthew 1:5-16). Her acceptance of the God of Israel and her obedience to His direction through Naomi results in great blessing from Him.

Personalize this lesson.

☑ When Naomi and Ruth left Moab and set out for Bethlehem, they did not know how their story would turn out. For all they knew, they would remain widows and scrape for food and shelter for years to come. Naomi, especially, did not hide her sadness and despair; even so, she reflected God's character well enough to Ruth that Ruth was able to trust implicitly in God. We, of course, know that God had tremendous blessing and restoration waiting for them, through a righteous man who embraced God's law even in a time of widespread lawlessness.

Like Ruth and Naomi, we are often faced with needing to move forward when we cannot see how our stories will turn out. We may not see God working. We may not see how circumstances could change. Yet that does not mean that the God who has committed to be our faithful Redeemer and Restorer has altered or that His commitment to us has wavered.

Even if we cannot see the outcome, we, too, will be rewarded for seeking and following the One who loves us with an everlasting love. Boaz's words to Ruth apply as well to us: *"The Lord repay you for what you have done, and a full reward be given you by the Lord, the God of Israel, under whose wings you have come to take refuge!"* (Ruth 2:12).

Lesson 3

Esther in the Persian Court

Esther 1:1-2:23

❖ Esther 1:1-9—King Ahasuerus's Banquet

1. Read the description of the banquet given in verses 5-8. What details of this event stand out to you?

2. What has happened immediately prior to the banquet?

3. What do verses 1-8 suggest to you about King Ahasuerus and the culture of his day?

4. Although Persian customs did not forbid wives from appearing at social occasions with their husbands, what special arrangements have been made for the women in this instance?

❖ Esther 1:10-22—Queen Vashti's Refusal

5. What command does the king give concerning the queen and why?

____

____

____

6. *For personal thought:* Remembering the context in which she acts, do you think Queen Vashti's refusal is justified? Why or why not?

____

____

____

7. Verse 12 says the king was *"enraged."* What do you think accounts for his reaction?

____

____

8. What line of reasoning do the king's *"wise men"* use about the queen's refusal?

____

____

9. Do you consider Memucan's recommendation to be sound? Why, or why not?

____

____

____

❖ Esther 2:1-11—Esther Is Brought to the Harem

10. How does the king begin the process for selecting a new queen?

____

____

11. What does this passage tell you about Esther's background, personal appearance, and character?

12. What insights do these verses provide into the relationship between Esther and Mordecai?

❖ Esther 2:12-18—A New Queen

13. How were the young virgins prepared for presentation to the king?

14. What happened to the young women after the king had spent the night with them?

15. What effect does Esther have on others, including the king?

❖ Esther 2:19-23—Mordecai Speaks Up

16. Mordecai has already been mentioned, but now he takes center stage. Scan chapter 2 again. What do you learn about Mordecai?

17. *For personal thought:* This is the second time Mordecai asked Esther not to reveal her Jewish heritage (2:10, 20). Why do you think Mordecai gave Esther this instruction?

18. How does Mordecai save the king's life?

19. *For personal thought:* From what we already know of Ahasuerus's character, does it seem surprising to you that Mordecai stepped in to prevent his assassination? Can you think of a reason he might have been tempted to keep quiet and let events take their natural course? Why do you think he did what he did? (See 1 Samuel 26:9-11; and 1 Peter 2:13, 17.)

Apply what you have learned. Vashti and Esther lived within a system that was degrading to women, and badly misrepresented God's intention for the way men and women should conduct themselves with one another. Vashti chose to resist the system—and lost her influence. Esther worked within the system—but is sometimes criticized for compromising. Have you ever been in a situation that demanded you to make tough choices similar to those Vashti and Esther were forced to make? Consider their stories, along with the following Scripture passages: Matthew 10:16; Romans 12:2; Ephesians 5:16; Colossians 4:5; James 1:5. What guidance do you receive from your study that could help you with similar future decisions?

Lesson 3 Commentary

Esther in the Persian Court

Esther 1:1-2:23

The book of Esther concerns Jewish exiles in Persia during the reign of King Ahasuerus. An incident in the Persian court places Persia's estimated 15 million Jews in jeopardy. Even today, at the Feast of Purim, Jews celebrate the salvation God brought through a young orphan named Esther.

We know little about the experience of the Jews in exile. The book of Esther is the only biblical account about the Jews during that time. Although some scholars have questioned the historicity of this book, recent scholarship validates its reliability. Herodotus, a Greek historian of the period, described a Persian culture exactly like that described in Esther.

Esther is the only book of the Bible that never mentions God. Yet God's providence is woven throughout the account. The miracle of Jewish survival in the Persian Empire and through the ages is an undeniable fact of history. God's sovereign ability to carry out His good plans can be an encouragement for all of us.

The Royal Banquet in Susa (Esther 1:1-22)

Ahasuerus succeeded his father Darius as king of the vast Persian Empire extending from the Indus river basin in India to the upper Nile region. Susa, located in the modern nation of Iran, was Ahasuerus's winter capital. A six-month display of the royal riches culminated in the seven-day banquet (1:3-5). Although Persian custom allowed wives to dine with their husbands, Queen Vashti gave a banquet for the women who were present (1:9). On the seventh day of this feasting, Ahasuerus wanted to show off beautiful Queen Vashti adorned with the royal crown. When she defied the king's request, he was *"enraged"* (1:12).

The king usually surrounded himself with men who were experts in the Law (see Ezra 7:1). These men made Vashti's refusal to appear at the king's request into a public and national crisis. These *"wise men"* (1:13) persuaded Ahasuerus that Vashti's example would influence women to disrespect their husbands and bring discord into families. So the king deposed Vashti and commanded women to learn from her and respect their husbands.

Esther Chosen as Queen (Esther 2:1-23)

"After these things" (2:1) suggests the passing of a number of years, which may have included Ahasuerus's failed military campaign against the Greeks from 482 to 479 BC. The events of chapter 2 took place upon his return. As Ahasuerus returned to Persia, he remembered Vashti at Susa (2:1). Perhaps to keep the king happy, his personal attendants proposed a plan to select a new queen. Pleased with their suggestions, Ahasuerus appointed a commission in every province to search for *"beautiful young virgins"* (2:2).

A Jew named Mordecai, from the tribe of Benjamin, lived in Susa. His ancestors were among the citizens of Jerusalem and Judah exiled to Babylon in 597 BC (2 Kings 24:8-17). Mordecai assumed parental responsibility for his orphaned cousin, Hadassah (a Hebrew name meaning *"myrtle"*), later known as Esther (a Persian name meaning *"star,"* or *"Ishtar,"* the Babylonian goddess of love). It was common for Hebrew exiles to have Babylonian or, later, Persian names as well as Hebrew names.

Living in the citadel of Susa, Mordecai could not hide Esther from the officers who were searching for beautiful girls to supply the royal harem. Esther immediately became a favorite of the eunuch in charge of the harem. He assigned seven maids to her, provided her with cosmetics and food, and gave her *"the best place in the harem"* (2:9). Concerned for Esther's welfare, Mordecai spent much time in the harem courtyard. He cautioned her not to reveal her family identity or nationality.

In 12 months, Esther completed the prescribed beauty treatments (2:12). Persia, India, and Arabia were known for their perfumes, which were exported to other countries and used lavishly at home. Archaeologists have found cosmetic burners used to saturate the skin and hair with fragrant fumes from aromatic spices.

When Esther was presented to the king, *"she won grace and favor in his sight"* (2:17). He was so pleased with Esther that he chose her to replace Vashti. Proclaiming a holiday, Ahasuerus gave a great banquet, presenting Esther as the queen of Persia before his nobles and officials.

Think about Mordecai and Esther's relationship to God. Scholars wonder how Esther could in good conscience conform to Persian court life. Could it be that Esther had not received typical Jewish religious training? Whether Mordecai and Esther were weak morally and spiritually we do not know, but they had strong personal ethics, risking their own lives to save their people and accomplish God's plan. The fact that they had weaknesses is exactly why we can relate to them. Esther illustrates how God reaches to us where we are and uses us despite our weaknesses.

Mordecai Uncovers a Plot (Esther 2:19-23)

The second assembling of the virgins (2:19) very likely occurred after the ceremonies elevating Esther as queen. The virgins may have been allowed to return home, but, more likely, the king kept them in his harem as concubines. The victims of this system endured separation from their families and, forbidden normal relationships with men, were doomed to a life of virtual widowhood.

"Mordecai was sitting at the king's gate" (2:19). Throughout the ancient Near East, officials, judges, and magistrates met inside these large gates to conduct business and administer the governmental affairs. Mordecai likely had been appointed as a magistrate or judge through Esther's influence.

When Mordecai learned of a plot to kill the king, he reported it to Esther, who in turn informed King Ahasuerus. More than one ruler has been killed by his own servants, and 14 years later a similar plot against Ahasuerus succeeded. Mordecai's report was investigated and the guilty officers were promptly hanged. The royal annals credited Mordecai with uncovering this conspiracy and saving the king's life.

Personalize this lesson.

☑ Esther probably would not have chosen to leave her uncle's family and enter the pagan king's harem. However, after being forced to go there, she demonstrated maturity, humility, and good sense. Like Esther, we face situations we would not choose, but we can control our responses to them. Where do circumstances have you these days? Are you fearful? Discouraged? Frustrated? Without hope? Tell God how you feel. Remind Him—and yourself—that He loves to work in the most unlikely situations. Ask Him for grace to walk humbly and to trust Him for the good He is going to do. Then watch and listen for signs of what He's up to so you can join Him in it, as Esther did.

Lesson 4

For Such a Time as This

Esther 3:1-4:17

Memorize God's Word: Esther 4:14.

❖ Esther 3:1-6—Haman's Plot

1. How is Haman identified in 3:1, 10; 8:3, 5; 9:24?

2. *For further study:* Skim 1 Samuel 15, Exodus 17:8-16, Deuteronomy 25:17-19, and 1 Chronicles 4:43. With whom is *"Agag"* associated? Describe the relationship between Israel and the nation mentioned in these texts.

3. What does this passage reveal about Haman's personality and character?

4. How does the background you considered in question 2 help you better understand Haman's attitude toward the Jews?

5. What does Mordecai do that angers Haman? Why do you think Mordecai did this?

6. After Mordecai offends him, what does Haman scheme to do?

7. In making his appeal to the king, what approach does Haman take?

❖ Esther 3:7-15—Providential Timing

8. How was the timing determined for when the Jews would be destroyed?

9. Compare 3:12 with Exodus 12:1-2 and Leviticus 23:5. What is the significance of the timing of Haman's edict?

10. Compare 3:7 with 3:12. How many months after the edict is given is it to be carried out? Now read Proverbs 16:33. In what ways do you see God's hand directing the timing of these events?

11. In verses 12-14, note how often the words *all* and *every* appear. How many Jews would remain in the kingdom if Haman's order were carried out exactly as prescribed?

12. How do the king and Haman respond after the decree is issued? How does the city of Susa respond? If you didn't know the end of the story, what predictions might you make based on what 3:15 reveals of these two men's attitudes?

❖ Esther 4:1-11—Esther's Challenge

13. We looked at the response of Ahasuerus, Haman, and the city of Susa to Haman's death-dealing edict. How did Mordecai and Esther respond?

14. What explanation and command did Mordecai give to Esther through Hathach when she sent him to learn about Mordecai's distress?

15. How do you interpret Esther's initial reaction to Mordecai's command?

16. Consider what happened to Vashti when she challenged the king in chapter one. Do you think Esther's reluctance was justified? Why or why not?

❖ Esther 4:12-17—Esther Makes Her Decision

17. Mordecai sends another message to Esther, trying again to move her to action. In your view, what part of his message in 4:13-14 is most persuasive?

18. After agreeing to Mordecai's command, Esther gives Mordecai a command of her own. What does she tell him to do?

19. Esther points out to Mordecai that his request is against the law. Nevertheless, she agrees to do it. What does her decision say about her faith?

Apply what you have learned. What character qualities do you admire in Esther? Is there one of these that you would like for God to help you develop in your life? Talk to Him about it. Ask Him to give you one step you can take to help you grow in this area—then trust Him to help you and do whatever He shows you.

Lesson 4 Commentary

For Such a Time as This

Esther 3:1-4:17

Haman Plots to Destroy the Jews (Esther 3)

Throughout Esther, Haman is referred to as *"Haman the Agagite"* (3:1, 10; 8:3, 5; 9:24). There are two possible interpretations of this reference. One is that Haman came from the province of Agag in Media. A second interpretation, which most commentators seem to prefer, is that Haman descended from Agag, king of the Amalekites. When Saul was king of Israel, God ordered him to completely destroy the Amalekites (1 Samuel 15:2-3). But Saul did not fully obey the Lord's command. He took King Agag alive.

Think about partial obedience. If Saul had fully obeyed God, the Jews would not have had to deal with Haman centuries later. God does not allow us to choose the portions of His commands we will obey. In Saul's case, the personal consequence of his rebellion was the loss of his throne. But, as is often true of disobedience, the consequences were more far-reaching than that. The estimated nearly 15 million Jews living in Esther's day were nearly annihilated because of Saul's partial obedience.

Haman became a favorite courtier of King Ahasuerus during the four years following Esther's selection as queen (see 2:16 and 3:7). The king commanded that all officials should honor Haman by kneeling before him. Mordecai, however, refused to pay such homage.

Why Mordecai refused to bow is not clear. Some commentators suggest that he refused in obedience to the Second Commandment (Exodus 20:5). However, it should be noted that it was not uncommon for Israelites to bow as a sign of respect (see Genesis 23:7; 33:3, 6-7; 42:6; 1 Samuel 24:8; 2 Samuel 14:4; 18:28; 1 Kings 1:16; 1 Chronicles 29:20). Whatever his reason, he seems to have asserted his identity as a Jew when asked by royal officials. This is interesting, as he instructed Esther not to reveal her Jewish identity. Haman's rage toward Mordecai spread to include the entire Jewish population. Consequently, he made plans to kill the Jews throughout the whole Persian Empire.

In the month of Nisan, the first month of the year, *"they cast the Pur (that is, they cast lots)"* (3:7). The *"Pur"* represents the Babylonian word *puru* (*"lot"* or *"fate"*). The lot fell on the 13th day of the 12th month (3:7, 13). Although this gave the Jews 11 months to plan, the Persians would not have considered altering the date selected by casting the lot.

After he determined the date, Haman sought Ahasuerus's permission to destroy the Jews. While not identifying them explicitly to the king, he described the moral, civil, and ceremonial laws that separated them from Persian society (see Deuteronomy 4:8). To charge the Jews with disobeying the king's laws, however, was a diabolical perversion of facts. That Ahasuerus did not ask who these people were before he gave permission for their destruction reveals much about his character.

"On the thirteenth day of the first month" (3:12) Haman finalized the plans and had them announced. Ironically—yet *providentially*—this date was the eve of the Jewish Passover (Exodus 12:1-2; Leviticus 23:5). With this terrible announcement fresh in their minds, what must Passover have been like for faithful Jews *that* year?

The king's scribes soon issued the edict *"to destroy, to kill, and to annihilate all the Jews, young and old, women and children ... and to plunder their goods"* (3:13). The Jews had prospered in exile, so the plundering and confiscation of property was significant. Perhaps the edict was even issued long in advance in the hope that many Jews would flee, leaving their property behind. While the residents of Susa were *"thrown into confusion"* by this edict, *"the king and Haman sat down to drink"* (3:15). What a dramatic contrast!

Esther Makes Her Decision (Esther 4)

Mordecai tore his clothes when he *"learned all that had been done"* (4:1). Perhaps he felt responsible because he had revealed his nationality to royal officials, ultimately bringing Haman's wrath upon all the Jews (3:4). He showed his anguish publicly by appearing in sackcloth, wailing loudly and bitterly near the king's gate. Jews all over the empire reacted likewise, *"fasting and weeping and lamenting"* (4:3). Public expression of grief was customary in that day. Tearing the clothes and wearing sackcloth and ashes are mentioned many places in the Old Testament (e.g., Genesis 37:34; Ezekiel 27:30-33).

It seems that everyone in the kingdom—except Queen Esther and the women in the royal harem—knew about the edict. When the servants told the queen about Mordecai's public appearance in sackcloth, she did not understand. Esther sent Mordecai clothing to replace his coarse, rough sackcloth. When he refused these, she sent Hathach, one of the king's eunuchs, to find out what was wrong.

Mordecai thoroughly briefed Hathach, telling him the *"exact sum of money that Haman had promised to pay into the king's treasuries for the destruction of the Jews"* (4:7). He gave Hathach a copy of the edict to show to Esther, urging that she appeal to the king for mercy.

Esther responded with fear for her safety. The polygamous monarch had not summoned her for 30 days. Furthermore, he had deposed the previous queen when she challenged his authority. Esther would risk her life if she took the initiative to see him and request the reversal of the decree. Mordecai's reply was brutally explicit: death for her, a Jewess, was certain if she did *not* appeal to the king. Mordecai was certain that help would come *"from another place"* for the Jews, but not for Esther if she failed in this opportunity. He challenged her with the piercing question: *"And who knows whether you have not come to the kingdom for such a time as this?"* (4:14).

Esther appealed to Mordecai for support in a three-day fast by the Jews in Susa. Fasting was normally accompanied by prayer. In this crisis, surely the Jews must have prayed, although it is not mentioned here.

Esther decided to approach the king. Her words did not show confidence in success as much as determination to try: *"If I perish, I perish"* (4:16).

Personalize this lesson.

☑ How do you see God working behind the scenes in this lesson? Is there a crisis or hardship in your life right now? Do you trust that God is working behind the scenes for you, too? Ask God if He might be willing to give you a glimpse of His behind-the-scenes watchfulness and care for you. Sit quietly with Him for a while, to allow Him to speak to you. Thank Him for whatever He reveals. Then ask Him for faith to trust Him more—even when you can't see the outcome.

Lesson 5

Pride and Prejudice

Esther 5:1-7:10

❖ Esther 5:1-8—Esther Approaches the King

1. Why was approaching the king as Esther did risky? Why do you suppose the king received Esther with such favor?

2. Read Hebrews 4:14-16. Contrast the likelihood of Esther gaining an audience with the king to the likelihood we have of gaining an audience with the King of kings. How and why are the two situations different? How do these differences affect your desire to approach God with your needs?

3. What are possible reasons Esther may have chosen to delay revealing her request by an additional day?

❖ Esther 5:9-14—Haman Plots Mordecai's Death

4. What was Haman's mood as he left Esther's feast?

5. What triggered a change of attitude for him?

6. What did Haman brag about to his friends and his wife later that day? What kept him from enjoying all these "successes"?

7. What did Haman's wife suggest Haman do to deal with his ill humor?

❖ Esther 6:1-14—Ahasuerus Honors Mordecai

8. What problem did the king experience the night following Esther's first banquet?

9. What remedy did he turn to, and what surprising turn of events resulted?

10. How do you see God acting behind the scenes in these events?

Esther 7:1-10—Esther Reveals Haman's Plot

11. Finally, Esther tells the king her request. What is it, and what reasoning does she use?

12. Take a moment to reflect on Esther's strategy in attempting to rescue her people from Haman's evil plot. What character qualities does she exhibit that you admire?

13. Granted, Haman did not have the benefit of Scripture. But if he had, how could the following verses have protected him from making such fatal mistakes?

    a. Numbers 32:23

    b. Psalm 7:14-16

    c. Proverbs 11:2

    d. Proverbs 16:18

    e. Galatians 6:7

14. *For personal thought:* Does one of the verses you considered in the previous question contain wisdom you need currently? Which one? How does it apply?

15. Reflect on the story of Esther so far. Make a list of all the seeming coincidences that actually were the means God used to deliver His people. For example, Queen Vashti was deposed, so a new queen had to be found. This positioned Esther for the work God had for her.

16. Have you seen God work on your behalf through seemingly random circumstances (that to Him were not random at all!)? If so, how have you seen Him work like this?

Apply what you have learned. Prejudice led to Haman's downfall. Haman's prejudice was blatant, but there can be more subtle forms. Do you avoid people who are in a higher or lower social class than you? Are you as welcoming to disabled people as you are to those who do not have limitations? Are you uncomfortable around people who have a different educational background from yours? A "yes" to one of these questions may indicate a seed of prejudice. Ask God to help you love people who are different from you. Then, intentionally reach out to somebody who is not like you. Even a simple greeting and smile can be a good start.

Lesson 5 Commentary

Pride and Prejudice

Esther 5:1-7:10

Esther Seeks an Audience With the King (Esther 5:1-14)

After fasting for three days, Esther put on her royal robes and ventured before King Ahasuerus. When the king saw Esther he was pleased and extended his scepter, accepting her. The king promised to grant whatever she requested *"even to the half of my kingdom"* (5:3). Such an offer was never taken lightly. Esther's request was simple. She invited Ahasuerus and Haman for a banquet she had prepared for them on that very day.

During the banquet, Ahasuerus once more questioned Esther about her request. Surprisingly, she delayed again and invited the king and Haman for another banquet. This delay posed a risk. Haman might discover Esther's identity as a Jewess, or the king's schedule might force cancellation.

Haman left the banquet *"joyful and glad of heart"* (5:9) … until he met Mordecai at the gate. Mordecai *"neither rose nor trembled before him"* (5:9), and Haman went home enraged. That evening he boasted to his family and friends about the honors bestowed upon him. Yet seeing Mordecai spoiled his joy.

His wife and friends advised Haman to build gallows for Mordecai's execution. They assured Haman that if he had Mordecai hanged the next morning, he would be able to fully enjoy the banquet. He gave orders immediately for the erection of gallows 75 feet high, approximately as high as the city wall.

The Tables Turn (Esther 6:1-13)

"That night the king could not sleep" (6:1). The king's insomnia resulted in developments that unfolded so favorably for the Jews that many readers see the events as miraculous or even fabricated. Unable to sleep,

Ahasuerus requested his servants read the royal diary to him. They read through the night until they came to Mordecai's report of the two conspirators (2:23).

The Persians kept detailed records of all the affairs of state and the royal family. Exceptional service to the king was recorded and rewarded, but Ahasuerus could not recall what had been done for Mordecai. The next morning he asked: *"What honor or distinction has been bestowed on Mordecai?"* (6:3). Told that none had been given, he asked who might suggest how Mordecai could be honored properly; not rewarding one who had saved the king's life was a serious matter. Ironically, Haman had just entered the court, hoping for the king's permission to have Mordecai hanged. He was brought before the king, who asked his advice (6:6). Thinking the king intended to honor him, Haman proposed an extravagant plan. The honored man should wear royal apparel and ride on the king's horse. One of the king's most noble princes should lead the honoree through the streets of Susa, proclaiming, *"Thus shall it be done to the man whom the king delights to honor"* (6:9).

Imagine Haman's shock and horror when King Ahasuerus ordered Haman to honor Mordecai in this way! After this painful, humiliating parade through the streets, Haman returned home. Haman covered his head in mourning (6:12), showing that he realized how precarious his situation was. He recounted the turn of events to his wife and friends. His friends were not helpful. They had known Mordecai was a Jew when they advised building the gallows for his hanging (5:13-14). Now they said, *"If Mordecai … is of the Jewish people, you will not overcome him"* (6:13). They were aware that the Jews experienced some sort of special protection.

Think about how pride was Haman's undoing and his primary sin. From it sprang another common sin: prejudice. To be prejudiced is to hold a preconceived bias, usually negative, about a person or group of people. Sometimes it feels good to think we are better than another; it feeds our egos.

In Jesus' day, Jews were prejudiced toward Samaritans, often walking many extra miles to avoid contact with them. Jesus, however, walked straight through their country. There He showed loving acceptance of a Samaritan woman, a social outcast. Count the number of prejudices He ignored in that one encounter!

Have you felt the sting of prejudice against you? Consider Jesus' example, which shows how God views even the lowliest person. No matter what injustice you suffer from others, God sees you as of immense worth and importance—a valuable creation of God the Creator.

Esther Appeals for Her People (Esther 7:1-10)

As the king and Haman dined at Esther's banquet, Ahasuerus once more asked about her request. He addressed her as Queen Esther, a sign of royal favor. Encouraged, she bravely made her request: *"Let my life be granted me ... and my people .... For we have been sold, I and my people, to be destroyed, to be killed, and to be annihilated"* (7:3-4).

Esther's dramatic plea shocked the king, who was unaware of her Jewish identity. She continued by saying that she and her people were being sold for annihilation—perhaps even sharing with the king the exact price Haman had paid (4:7). If she and her people were to be sold into slavery it might be one thing, but she could not keep silent when their final destiny was involved.

When King Ahasuerus asked who dared to do such a thing, Esther pointed to Haman (7:6). Enraged, Ahasuerus strode out to the palace garden. Haman, sensing his fate was already decided, threw himself on Esther's mercy, literally *"falling on the couch where Esther was"* (7:8). How ironic that Haman, furious when the Jew Mordecai refused to bow down (3:2), now fell down before the Jewess Esther! When Ahasuerus returned, he reacted to the scene, exclaiming, *"Will he even assault the queen in my presence, in my own house?"* (7:8). There were strict rules concerning the royal harem. Kneeling even a foot away from the couch was punishable by death.

Attendants quickly covered Haman's face before the raging king. Harbona, an attending eunuch, said that gallows had been erected at Haman's house for the execution of Mordecai. With no hesitation, the king ordered that Haman be executed on the same gallows. *"Then the wrath of the king abated"* (7:10).

Personalize this lesson.

Haman aggressively sought his own promotion. Mordecai humbly did what was right, without concern for personal elevation. He overheard the plot to assassinate the king and saved Ahasuerus's life (2:19-23). His act was recorded in a book and forgotten—until God revealed it at just the perfect time. By their opposite attitudes, Haman and Mordecai illustrate the truth of Proverbs 18:12: *"Before destruction a man's heart is haughty, but humility comes before honor."* Is there a situation in your life now where God is calling you to have more of a Mordecai attitude? Tell God what it feels like to seem forgotten and overlooked. Pour out your heart to Him and lean on His care. Ask Him to help you wait for Him to give you the affirmation and recognition you need.

Lesson 6

A Happy Ending

Esther 8:1-10:3

❖ Esther 8:1-17—Esther Saves the Jews

1. Haman is dead, but the Jews' troubles are not over. Why not? (Review 3:12-14.)

2. Esther appears unbidden before the king once again. How is this appearance different from her previous one (5:1-2)? What do you think accounts for these differences?

3. What does Esther request of the king this time?

4. In what way is this request problematic for the king? (See Esther 1:19; 3:12; 8:8; Daniel 6:8, 12.)

5. How is the problem resolved?

6. What does the king do that suggests Mordecai now holds the place of honor Haman previously held?

____

____

7. Esther is just one of many godly Jewish men and women who have interceded for the lives of their people. Read the scriptures below and note who interceded and for what.

   a. Exodus 32:1-14 ______________________________

   ____

   ____

   b. Ezra 9:1-15 ______________________________

   ____

   ____

   c. Nehemiah 1:1-11 ______________________________

   ____

   ____

   d. I Kings 18:30-39 ______________________________

   ____

   ____

   e. Daniel 9:1-19 ______________________________

   ____

   ____

8. How did the Jews *"in every province and in every city"* respond when they heard about the second decree?

____

____

9. *For deeper thought:* Contrast 2:10 with the second part of 8:17. How would you explain the differences you observe?

____

____

❖ Esther 9:1-32—The Jews Defend Themselves

10. Verses 1-10 describe a reversal for the Jews. Think over the whole of Esther. What are some details of this reversal?

11. What tradition does Mordecai announce in the letters he sends to Jews in all the provinces?

12. How is this new tradition to be observed? What is it named?

13. *For personal thought:* What victories has God won for you or your family? How could you commemorate and celebrate these acts of deliverance?

❖ Esther 10:1-3—Mordecai Is Elevated

14. What position does Mordecai hold in the Persian Empire?

15. We can gain much wisdom from reflecting on others' lives. What can you learn from:

    a. Haman? ______

    b. Mordecai? ______

    c. Esther? ______

16. *For personal thought:* Is there one thing from each of their lives that you would like to apply to your life?

17. Read Psalm 37:34-36. How do these verses apply to these three people? Is there a way God might be inviting you to apply these verses?

Apply what you have learned. How does Esther's example of intercession, along with the examples you read about in question 7, inspire you? Who among "your people" (e.g., your relatives, church, city, organization) needs your intercession? Ask God how He would like you to pray for these people, and ask for His creative ideas about how you could pray more intentionally.

Lesson 6 Commentary

A Happy Ending

Esther 8:1-10:3

Mordecai and Esther Find Favor (Esther 8:1-17)

When criminals were executed in the Persian Empire, the king decided how their property would be dispersed. Ahasuerus decided to give Haman's estate to Queen Esther. Furthermore, Ahasuerus made Mordecai one of his chief officers. Haman's power and prestige now belonged to Mordecai.

Yet the Jews still were not safe. Esther made another, strikingly different, appeal to the king. Esther had called upon the dignity of her position to make her first request; now she *"fell at his feet and wept and pleaded with him"* (8:3). Ahasuerus held out the scepter to her, inviting her request. Esther begged the king to write an order overruling Haman's edict.

The king could not grant Esther's request. By law, any edict issued using the king's seal and name could not be revoked (see 1:19; Daniel 6:8, 12, 15). Ahasuerus extricated himself from this bind by authorizing Mordecai to issue a new order authorizing the Jews to destroy anyone who attacked them and to confiscate their property. They had eight months to prepare *"to take vengeance on their enemies"* (8:13). The fateful day was set for March 7, 473 BC, the same day chosen by Haman for the annihilation of the Jews (3:13).

Couriers distributed the new decree throughout the 127 provinces of the empire (8:9). Mordecai then appeared in Susa dressed in royal attire and received great acclaim from the people. *"The city of Susa shouted and rejoiced"* (8:15) in response to the decree. It was a time of genuine gladness for the Jews far and near. In every city and province their mourning became rejoicing, their fasting changed to feasting. The incredible reversal resulted in many people converting to Judaism, as *"fear of the Jews had fallen on them"* (8:17).

The Great Reversal (Esther 9:1-32)

When the day finally arrived, the Jews defended themselves with extraordinary success. Some historians suggest there may have been 15 million Jews living among a total population of perhaps 100 million. If numbers were what mattered, the numbers were against the Jews. But numbers mean nothing when God is in control.

In Susa the Jews killed 500 people and the 10 sons of Haman. When this was reported to Ahasuerus, he asked Esther if she had a further petition. She requested his approval for another day to carry out the edict, perhaps to ensure that any remaining opposition was dealt with. The king granted her request, and 300 more men were killed in Susa. Also, the bodies of Haman's 10 sons were hung in public view. In the Hebrew text, the names of these sons are traditionally printed in perpendicular type—illustrating the shape of a gallows.

It is noteworthy that the Jews *"laid no hands on the plunder"* (9:10, 15-16). Perhaps they were not interested in retaliation as much as basic self-defense. Throughout the provinces, the Jews who assembled to protect themselves limited their activities to only one day, killing about 75,000 people.

Think about Although Mordecai's new edict gave the Jews the right to plunder any enemy who attacked them, they chose not to exercise this right. We see this same attitude in Jesus. He laid aside His rights as God. Rather than look to His own interests, He looked to ours and became a humble servant (Philippians 2:4, 6). As believers, we are to do things that build others up, not merely satisfy our own desires (1 Corinthians 10:23). God might invite you to give up something you are rightfully entitled to. If you accept His invitation, you can be sure that you will bring Him joy. Why? Because you will remind Him of His Son, Jesus!

The day after this remarkable deliverance, the Jews *"rested and made it a day of feasting and joy"* (9:17). Sending letters to the Jews far and near, Mordecai declared the 14th and 15th of Adar to be annual days of celebration. Queen Esther sent a second letter that established the feast of Purim with fasting and lamenting (9:31). Evidently, Esther considered fasting such a vital part in the deliverance that she wanted it to be a part of the Purim observance.

Since Haman had determined the day for their destruction when he cast the *"Pur,"* or lot (9:24), the Jews called these days of celebration Purim (plural of the Hebrew word *pur*). For millennia Jews have observed the Feast of Purim. The 13th day of Adar (March 7, 473 BC) is observed as "Esther's fast" before the joyous celebration of Purim on the 14th and 15th. Usually the scroll of Esther is read in its traditional chant. Feasting, rejoicing, and sharing of gifts make this a joyous celebration.

Mordecai Is Elevated (Esther 10:1-3)

Mordecai is now honored and elevated. We remember where he started—a lowly, despised outcast caring for a young relative—but now the king has advanced him to second in rank to himself. He was *"great among the Jews ... for he sought the welfare of his people and spoke peace to all his people"* (10:3).

Like Joseph and Daniel, Mordecai lived as a foreigner in a foreign land and did not resign himself to victim status. Instead, he sought the good of those living in this place, as God had commanded in Jeremiah 29:7: *"Seek the welfare of the city where I have sent you into exile, and pray ... on its behalf, for in its welfare you will find your welfare."* Mordecai had done this. God had seen to his welfare, to Esther's welfare, and through them to the welfare of the entire Jewish people.

In contrast to Haman who sought to promote himself, we remember 1 Peter 5:5-6: *"Humble yourselves, therefore, under the mighty hand of God so that at the proper time He may exalt you."* God reversed the hardship, opposition, and humbling that Mordecai had experienced earlier in his life. At the right time, God positioned two unlikely people, Mordecai and Esther, to step into positions of extraordinary influence and play key roles in His providential plan for His people. Truly, they had both come to positions of power for *"such a time as this"* (4:14).

Personalize this lesson.

God established many feasts and fasts to commemorate His work among the Israelites. Passover, the Feast of Unleavened Bread, Pentecost, the Feast of Tabernacles, the Feast of First Fruits, the Feast of Trumpets, and the Day of Atonement are special observances God initiated. God did not command Purim and Hanukkah. Yet all were connected with God's work among His people and their response to His goodness toward them. Psalm 77:11 says, *"I will remember the deeds of the Lord."*

Even today, God's work in and through the lives of Ruth and Esther is remembered during the yearly feasts the Jews celebrate. What deeds has God done for you? How has He used you in the lives of others? What could you do to notice, remember, and celebrate God's obvious and not-so-obvious work in your life? Consider keeping a journal of what He has done, creating a "remembrance box" in which to keep mementos, or even throwing a yearly "feast" for friends or family in order to tell stories of God's work throughout that year. How could you more intentionally commemorate these deeds personally, or help your family or church to celebrate?

Small Group Leader's Guide

While *Engaging God's Word* is great for personal study, it is generally even more effective and enjoyable when studied with others. Studying with others provides different perspectives and insights, care, prayer support, and fellowship that studying on your own does not. Depending on your personal circumstances, consider studying with your family or spouse, with a friend, in a Sunday school, with a small group at church, work, or in your neighborhood, or in a mentoring relationship.

In a traditional Community Bible Study class, your study would involve a proven four-step method: personal study, a small group discussion facilitated by a trained leader, a lecture covering the passage of Scripture, and a written commentary about the same passage. *Engaging God's Word* provides two of these four steps with the study questions and commentary. When you study with a group, you add another of these—the group discussion. And if you enjoy teaching, you could even provide a modified form of the fourth, the lecture, which in a small group setting might be better termed a wrap-up talk.

Here are some suggestions to help leaders facilitate a successful group study.

1. Decide how long you would like each group meeting to last. For a very basic study, without teaching, time for fellowship, or group prayer, plan on one hour. If you want to allow for fellowship before the meeting starts, add at least 15 minutes. If you plan to give a short teaching, add 15 or 20 minutes. If you also want time for group prayer, add another 10 or 15 minutes. Depending on the components you include for your group, each session will generally last between one and two hours.
2. Set a regular time and place to meet. Meeting in a church classroom or a conference room at work is fine. Meeting in a home is also a good option, and sometimes more relaxed and comfortable.
3. Publicize the study and/or personally invite people to join you.

4. Begin praying for those who have committed to come. Continue to pray for them individually throughout the course of the study.
5. Make sure everyone has his or her own book at least a week before you meet for the first time.
6. Encourage group members to read the first lesson and do the questions before they come to the group meeting.
7. Prepare your own lesson.
8. Prepare your wrap-up talk, if you plan to give one. Here is a simple process for developing a wrap-up talk:
    a. Divide the passage you are studying into two or three divisions. Jot down the verses for each division and describe the content of each with one complete sentence that answers the question, "What is the passage about?"
    b. Decide on the central idea of your wrap-up talk. The central idea is the life-changing principle found in the passage that you believe God wants to implant in the hearts and minds of your group. The central idea answers the question, "What does God want us to learn from this passage?"
    c. Provide one illustration that would make your central idea clear and meaningful to your group. This could be an illustration from your own life, or a story you've read or heard somewhere else.
    d. Suggest one application that would help your group put the central idea into practice.
    e. Choose an aim for your wrap-up talk. The aim answers the question, "What does God want us to do about it?" It encourages specific change in your group's lives, if they choose to respond to the central idea of the passage. Often it takes the form of a question you will ask your group: "Will you, will I choose to ... ?"

9. Show up early to the study so you can arrange the room, set up the refreshments (if you are serving any), and welcome people as they arrive.
10. Whether your meeting includes a fellowship time or not, begin the discussion time promptly each week. People appreciate it when you respect their time. Transition into the discussion with prayer, inviting God to guide the discussion time and minister personally to each person present.
11. Model enthusiasm to the group. Let them know how excited you are about what you are learning—and your eagerness to hear what God is teaching them.
12. As you lead through the questions, encourage everyone to participate, but don't force anyone. If one or two people tend to dominate the discussion, encourage quieter ones to participate by saying something like, "Let's hear from someone who hasn't shared yet." Resist the urge to teach during discussion time. This time is for your group to share what they have been discovering.
13. Try to allow time after the questions have been discussed to talk about the "Apply what you have learned," "Think about" and "Personalize this lesson" sections. Encourage your group members in their efforts to partner with God in allowing Him to transform their lives.
14. Transition into the wrap-up talk, if you are doing one (see number 8).
15. Close in prayer. If you have structured your group to allow time for prayer, invite group members to pray for themselves and one another, especially focusing on the areas of growth they would like to see in their lives as a result of their study. If you have not allowed time for group prayer, you as leader can close this time.
16. Before your group finishes their final lesson, start praying and planning for what your next *Engaging God's Word* study will be.

Million+ people are engaging with God and His Word through CBS

Community Bible Study (CBS) is a global, interdenominational Bible study ministry offering a wide range of courses exploring various books of the Bible in both written and spoken formats, for all ages. Currently available in more than 85 languages, CBS Bible studies impact lives across more than 110 countries worldwide.

Since 1975, CBS has served as a conduit for the transformative power of God's Word; our participants study the Bible together in diverse settings, such as churches, prisons, schools, refugee camps, homes, coffee shops, and on the Internet. CBS is a participation-based ministry with trained leaders who foster in-depth, holistic engagement with God's Word within the context of a caring community, both in person and online.

The vision of Community Bible Study is, "Transformed Lives Through the Word of God."

The mission of Community Bible Study is, "To make disciples of the Lord Jesus Christ in our communities through caring, in-depth Bible Study, available to all."

CBS makes every effort to stand in the center of mainstream historic Christianity, concentrating on the essentials of the Christian faith rather than denominational distinctives. CBS respects different theological views, preferring to focus on helping people know God through His Word, grow deeper in their relationship with Jesus, and be transformed into His likeness.

Are you ready to go deeper in God's Word?

We would love to have you join us for an in-person or online CBS group. Scan the QR code to find a group.

For more information call 1-719-955-7777 or email info@communitybiblestudy.org.

Engage Bible Studies are available from Amazon and fine bookstores near you.

Scan the QR code to see all the available titles.

www.ingramcontent.com/pod-product-compliance
Lightning Source LLC
LaVergne TN
LVHW010543100826
845148LV00013B/2577

* 9 7 8 1 6 2 1 9 4 0 1 7 3 *